How to Learn
NEW WORDS

Book A
A Weekly Reader ® Skills Book

W9-CHS-654

Contents

Writer: Rita A. D'Apice
Senior Editor: Thomas J. Mooney
Consultant: William Page
Designer: Daria C. Holowaty
Illustrator: Blanche Sims
Cover Art: Blanche Sims
Copy Editor: Teresa A. Fucini
Senior Editorial Coordinator: Patricia M. Kneller
Publisher: Richard LeBrasseur

Recycled Paper

How to Learn
NEW WORDS

Strategies for Building Vocabulary

Book A

A
Weekly Reader®
Skills Book

To the Teacher

How To Learn New Words, *Weekly Reader's* five-book series for students in grades two through six, is designed to do exactly what its name implies—to teach students how to learn new words. Book A is designed to be used with students in grade two and above.

In **How To Learn New Words,** Book A, students learn how to:

- relate their current word knowledge to the context in which they discover an unfamiliar word;
- use context clues, such as definitions, examples, synonyms, antonyms, and descriptions to find the meaning of an unfamiliar word;
- use the meanings of prefixes and suffixes to bring precise meaning to words.

Using This Book

How To Learn New Words may be used with individual students, small groups of children, or an entire class. Each student should have his or her own book. It is essential to the success of the program that the teacher introduce each lesson so students have a clear understanding of new material. However, after a lesson is introduced and discussed, students may complete the exercises independently.

How To Learn New Words, Book A, is divided into 12 lessons. Each lesson is divided into four activities. There are also eight test pages in the book to check students' mastery of skills covered.

Be sure to preview each lesson before using it. You may wish to complete one lesson per week by assigning one activity per day and testing formally or informally on the fifth day. Or you may wish to spread a lesson out over a longer period of time. Adjust the pace to suit the ability of your group.

Use these follow-on activities to enhance your teaching of **How To Learn New Words.**

- After each lesson, have a vocabulary bee using words learned so far.
- Invite youngsters to share with classmates any new and interesting words they come across in their independent reading. Encourage children to write these interesting words on their word lists (page 45).
- In Book A, students learn about dictionaries. Have dictionaries available, and take time to teach youngsters beginning dictionary skills.
- Read stories that contain unfamiliar words. Have youngsters guess at meanings of the words, then check them out in a dictionary.
- Place dictionaries and a supply of crossword and other word puzzles in a learning center. Encourage youngsters to do the puzzles and to create their own word puzzles for classmates to solve.

Copyright © 1988 by Weekly Reader Corporation. All rights reserved. *Weekly Reader* is a federally registered trademark of Weekly Reader Corporation. Publishing, Executive, and Editorial Offices: 245 Long Hill Road, Middletown, CT 06457-9291. Subscription Offices: 3001 Cindel Drive, Delran, NJ 08370. Printed in U.S.A. Material in this book may not be reproduced; stored in a retrieval system; or transmitted in any form or by any means, electronic, mechanical, photocopying, or other, without special permission from the publisher.

ISBN: 0-8374-1751-1   8/96

Meet Jack-In-The-Box

Hi, <u>Girls and Boys</u>! My name is Jack. I <u>dwell</u> in a box. I keep words in my box. Whenever I learn a new word, I flip my lid.

In this book I'll teach you <u>lots</u> of ways to learn new words. Soon you'll be flipping your lids over each word you learn <u>too</u>. Now let's <u>peek</u> at some words I took out of my Word Box and listed in Activity 1.

Activity 1

Study the words. Then go back to the paragraphs at the beginning of this lesson. Match each underlined word to the word below that has the same meaning.

many _____

look _____

live _____

also _____

children _____

Activity 2

Now find and circle each word you learned in **Activity 1** in the Word Search puzzle. The words go across and down. One is done for you.

```
V  B  O  Y  S  A  K  V
G  X  D  W  E  L  L  C
I  L  O  T  S  S  O  L
R  I  X  V  T  O  O  A
L  V  Q  P  E  E  K  Z
S  E  M  A  N  Y  W  X
C  H  I  L  D  R  E  N
```

1

Learn About

Synonyms

Words that have the same meanings are called *synonyms* (SIN-ə-nim). Whenever you learn a new word, try to think of a synonym for that word.

Activity 3

Look at the words in my Word Box. They are synonyms for the **boldfaced** word under each sentence that follows.

> **Word Box**
>
> great, field, pretty, town, bandit, wagon, wise, large, woods, afraid

Read the sentences. Write a synonym from the Word Box for each **boldfaced** word.

1. A big, bad wolf lives deep in the king's _____ .
   forest
2. The people in the town were _____ of the wolf.
   scared
3. The _____ prince caught the big, bad wolf.
   clever
4. At the ball the prince met a _____ princess.
   beautiful
5. The king and queen lived in a _____ castle.
   huge
6. The king rode his horse through the little _____ .
   village
7. The queen's horse was grazing in the _____ .
   pasture
8. It was a _____ day for the prince's birthday party.
   terrific
9. A _____ tried to steal the king's gold.
   thief
10. The little old man wheeled the _____ of hay through the village.
    cart

> **Jack-in-the-Box's rule number 1 for learning words:** Learn synonyms for the words you know.

2

Synonym
Crossword Puzzle

Activity 4

Look at the words in the Word Box. They are synonyms for words you have learned.

Now read the word meanings below the crossword puzzle. Then choose a synonym from the Word Box for each word. Write that synonym in the puzzle. Remember, synonyms are words that have the same meanings. Be sure to follow the numbers across and down. The letters in the puzzle will help you.

> **Word Box**
>
> town, wagon, peek, bandit, scared, children, pasture, clever, many, also, beautiful, forest, huge, terrific, dwell

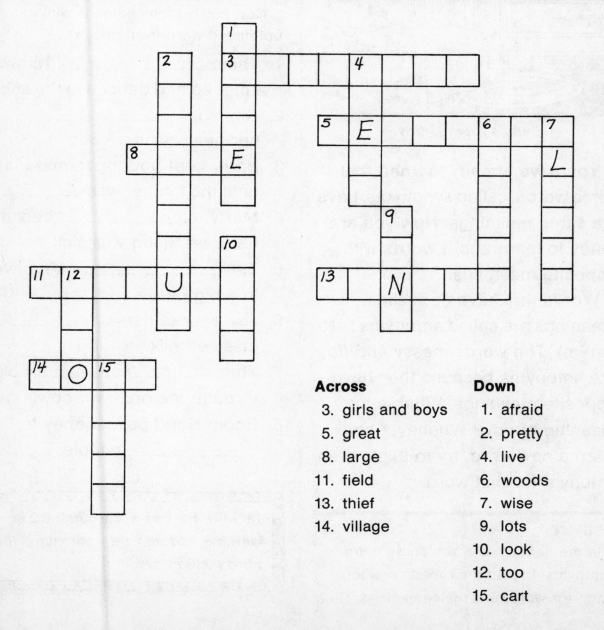

Across

3. girls and boys
5. great
8. large
11. field
13. thief
14. village

Down

1. afraid
2. pretty
4. live
6. woods
7. wise
9. lots
10. look
12. too
15. cart

Learn About
Antonyms

*Betty's room is **messy.***

*Betty's room is **tidy.***

You have already learned that some words, called synonyms, have the **same** meanings. Now you are ready to learn about words with **opposite** meanings.

Words that have opposite meanings are called *antonyms* (AN-tə-nim). The words *messy* and *tidy* are antonyms because they have opposite meanings. What is the meaning of *tidy?* Whenever you learn a new word, try to think of an antonym for that word.

Activity 1

In the next column are some pairs of antonyms. I listed their meanings too. Study the words and their meanings. Then follow the directions after the meanings.

1. **empty**—with nothing in it
   full—holding as much as possible
2. **merry**—full of fun
   sad—unhappy
3. **poor**—having very little money
   wealthy—having a lot of money
4. **warm**—slightly hot
   cool—slightly cold

Now finish each sentence with a **boldfaced** word from above.

1. The _____ old clown laughed and danced in the show.
2. Ginny felt _____ in her heavy winter coat.
3. Barry kept pouring lemonade until the pitcher was _____ .
4. Marty felt _____ because her best friend was sick.
5. The _____ king lived in a big castle.
6. Joy poured herself a _____ glass of milk.
7. The _____ air blew through the open window.
8. Robin Hood gave money to _____ people.

Jack-in-the-Box's rule number 2 for learning words: Learn antonyms for words you know.

Learn More
Antonyms

Look at the antonym pairs in my Word Box. I have listed the meaning of one word in each pair for you in each sentence below. It's up to you to figure out the meanings of the other words. Think you can do it? Let's try. Just remember that antonyms have opposite meanings.

Word Box
crooked—straight
strong—weak
wide—narrow
pretty—ugly
start—complete

Activity 2

Underline the meaning of the **boldfaced** word in each sentence.

1. If crooked means bent or twisted, then **straight** means
   not full   not curved   funny
2. If strong means powerful, then **weak** means
   a time of day   being late
            without strength
3. If wide means far apart, then **narrow** means
   close together   a short nap
            unhappy

4. If pretty means nice to look at, then **ugly** means
   not tall   not beautiful
            not covered
5. If start means to begin, then **complete** means
   to drive   to finish   to fly

Activity 3

Now practice spelling each new word. Write all the words in the Word Box in the puzzle. The words go across and down. The letter clues will help you.

Which word from the Word Box is missing in the puzzle? Write that word here. _____

5

Antonym
Crossword Puzzle

Activity 4

Look at the words in the Word Box. They are antonyms for words you have learned.

Now read the word meanings beside the crossword puzzle. Choose an antonym from the Word Box for each word. Then write that antonym in the puzzle. Remember, antonyms are words that have opposite meanings. Be sure to follow the numbers across and down. The letters in the puzzle will help you.

Word Box

merry, strong, straight, warm, start, ugly, narrow, empty, wealthy

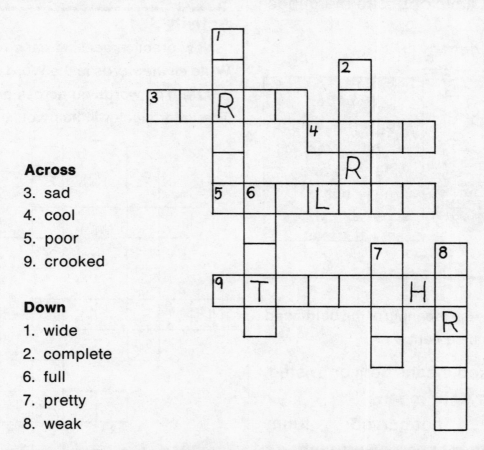

Across

3. sad
4. cool
5. poor
9. crooked

Down

1. wide
2. complete
6. full
7. pretty
8. weak

Now finish each sentence below with a word from the puzzle.

1. The _____ lady paid lots of money for a new plane.
2. Old King Cole was a _____ old soul.

3. I like to take long walks when the weather is _____ .
4. The Scouts hiked across the _____ footbridge.
5. Bart's piggy bank was _____ .

Practice
Using Synonyms and Antonyms

Activity 1

Study the pictures. Read the **boldfaced** words.

small or **tiny**   **gigantic**

wild or **fierce**   **tame**

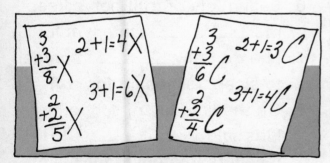

terrible or **awful**   **terrific**

smile or **grin**   **frown**

Now finish each sentence below with your choice of **boldfaced** words. Use the words only one time.

1. Bobby's pet raccoon is _____ .
2. Carol thought the roller coaster ride was _____ .
3. The birthday gift was too _____ to wrap.
4. That clown has a _____ on her face.
5. This banana tastes _____ .
6. I saw a _____ ant on the TV screen.
7. The animal trainer fed the _____ animals.
8. "It's time to go now," said Mother with a _____ on her face.

Just for fun, read your sentences to the class. How many different answers did you get? _____

> **Jack-in-the-Box's rule number 3 for learning words:** Try to figure out meanings of words you don't know from synonyms or antonyms of those words.

More Practice
Using Synonyms and Antonyms

Activity 2

Study the pictures. Read the **boldfaced** words.

sick or **ill**   **healthy**

fix or **repair**   **break**

cry or **sob**   **laugh**

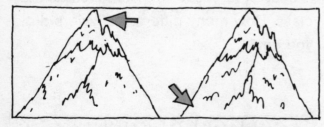

top or **peak**   **bottom**

good-bye or **farewell**   **hello**

Read the sentences below and the clue after each sentence. Then finish each sentence with the correct **boldfaced** word.

1. Dad likes to _____ old cars. (synonym for fix)
2. My baby sister doesn't _____ when she falls down. (antonym for laugh)
3. The cowboys left their horses at the _____ of the mountain. (antonym for peak)
4. My grandfather is _____. (synonym for sick)
5. All the Scouts at camp greeted one another with a friendly _____. (antonym for farewell)
6. Eating lots of fruit helps keep me _____. (antonym for ill)
7. I heard Sally _____ herself to sleep. (synonym for cry)
8. On the last day of school the kids said _____ to their teachers. (antonym for hello)
9. The mountain climber reached the _____ in four hours. (synonym for top)
10. I saw Henry _____ that pretty vase. (antonym for repair)

Synonym and Antonym
Word Search

Activity 3

Look at the words in the Word Box. They are words you have learned. First read the clues. Then write the correct synonym or antonym from the Word Box on each line.

Word Box

tiny, wild, bottom, hello, awful, small, healthy, frown, repair, top, cry, farewell

Clues

1. antonym for gigantic ___tiny___
2. synonym for fierce _____
3. synonym for terrible _____
4. synonym for tiny _____
5. antonym for grin _____
6. synonym for peak _____
7. antonym for break _____
8. synonym for sob _____
9. antonym for ill _____
10. synonym for good-bye _____
11. antonym for farewell _____
12. antonym for top _____

Now find words from the Word Box in the puzzle below. Circle each word you find. The words go across and down. The first one is done for you.

```
B  O  T  T  O  M  Y  Z
F  R  O  W  N  Y  H  X
A  W  P  P  A  T  E  Z
R  V  Q  Z  W  I  L  D
E  C  R  Y  F  N  L  F
W  X  X  V  U  Y  O  O
E  S  M  A  L  L  U  O
L  R  E  P  A  I  R  T
L  H  E  A  L  T  H  Y
```

Activity 4

Practice spelling synonyms and antonyms you have learned. Write words from the Word Box in the puzzle. The letter clues will help you.

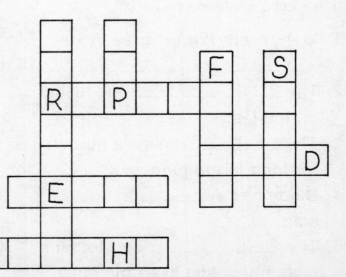

9

Show All You Know
About Synonyms and Antonyms

Draw lines to match each word below with a **synonym.**

peek	live
dwell	afraid
scared	look
town	pretty
beautiful	village

forest	also
too	robber
thief	woods
wise	cart
wagon	clever

Draw lines to match each word below with an **antonym.**

begin	complete
empty	sad
merry	cool
wealthy	full
warm	poor

crooked	pretty
smile	straight
ugly	frown
strong	weak

Word Box
field, tiny, wild, terrible, smile, narrow, gigantic, tame, frown

---

Choose words from the Word Box to finish each sentence below.

1. Many pretty flowers grew in the _____ .
2. The _____ bug rested on the leaf.
3. The _____ animals hunted for food in the jungle.
4. Cindy has a _____ cold.
5. The _____ on Mother's face meant she liked the gift.

Choose words from the Word Box to finish each sentence below.

1. We could see the _____ tree from far away.
2. The Scouts marched down the _____ path and into the woods.
3. We watched the _____ lions jump through hoops.
4. The _____ on my face told Dad I didn't like the soup.

Learn About
Prefixes

Many words that pop up from my Word Box have a *prefix* (PREE-fiks).

1. A prefix is a group of letters that has its own meaning.
   - *Dis-* is a prefix. *Dis-* means "not."
2. A prefix is added to the beginning of a word.
   - dis + obey = disobey
3. A prefix changes the meaning of a word.
   - *Obey* means "to follow orders." *Disobey* means "not to follow orders."

Activity 1

Make new words by adding the prefix *dis-* to each **boldfaced** word below. Then write a meaning for each word.

1. **continue**—to go on with
   discontinue—not to go on with

2. **honest**—truthful

   _____

3. **order**—neat

   _____

4. **agree**—to think the same

   _____

5. **like**—to care for something

   _____

Now finish each sentence below with a word you made.

1. Abe's room was a mess. Nothing was in order. Mom scolded Abe because his room was in such

   _____ .

2. Janet likes most everything but ice cream. The flavor she _____ the most is strawberry.

3. Beth thinks the color green is prettier than blue. Jason thinks blue is prettier than green. Those two friends seem to _____ about many things.

4. Ben cheated on the spelling test. Now everyone says Ben is

   _____ .

Learn More

About Prefixes

Now you know how the prefix *dis-* changes the meaning of a word. Other prefixes change word meanings too. *Re-* is a prefix. *Re-* means "again."

Example

Tell means "to say something."

Retell means "to tell, or say, something again."

Everyone wanted Mandy to retell the story about her lost kitten.

Activity 2

In my Word Box are words with the prefix *re-*. Read the words. Next read the sentences after the Word Box. Then finish each sentence with a word from the Word Box.

> **Word Box**
>
> refilled, replaced, reopen, retraced, reappear

1. Joe finished his milk and _____ his glass.

2. Mom _____ the flat tire on her car with a new one.

3. Andy's school will _____ in September.

4. In the play the elves disappear, then quickly _____ .

5. The rabbit _____ its tracks from the garden to its home in the woods.

Activity 3

Now go back to the Word Box. Draw a line between each prefix and the rest of the word. Then write the words in ABC (alphabetical) order on the lines below. The first one is done for you.

1. _____ re/appear _____
2. _____
3. _____
4. _____
5. _____

> **Jack-in-the-Box's rule number 4 for learning words:** Learn the meaning of *dis-* and *re-*. Remember how *dis-* and *re-* change word meanings.

Prefix
Crossword Puzzle Number 1

Activity 4

Look at the words in the Word Box. They are words you have learned with the prefixes *dis-* and *re-*.

Now read the word meanings below the crossword puzzle. Then choose a word from the Word Box that goes with each meaning. Write the word in the puzzle. Be sure to follow the numbers across and down. Letters in the puzzle will help you.

Word Box

disagree, disorder, reopen, reappear, refilled, dishonest, discontinue, retraced, replaced, dislike

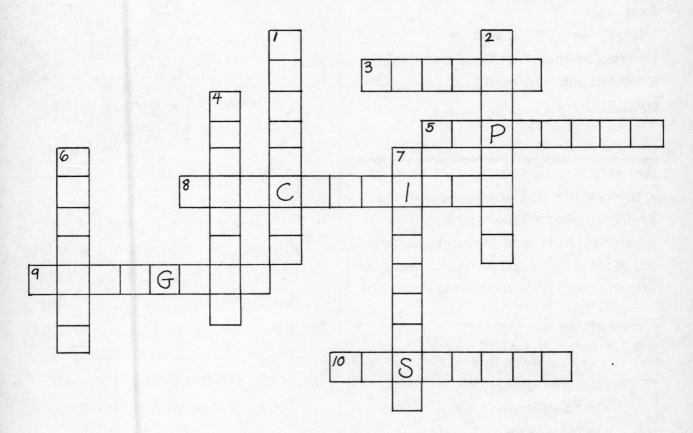

Across

3. open again
5. put something in place of another thing
8. not to go on doing something
9. not to think the same as someone else
10. mess; not in order

Down

1. go over lines on a paper again
2. come into sight again
4. filled again
6. not to care for something
7. not truthful

Learn About
The Prefix *un-*

Pop up and give yourself a cheer for learning about the prefixes *dis-* and *re-.* Now get ready to find out about the prefix *un-.*

You know that *dis-* means "not" and *re-* means "again." Guess what! The prefix *un-* also means "not."

Example

Happy means "filled with joy."
Unhappy means "not filled with joy."
Scott felt unhappy about not going to camp this year.

Activity 1

In my Word Box are words with the prefix *un-.* Read the words and their meanings. Next read the sentences after the Word Box. Then finish each sentence with the correct word from the Word Box.

> **Word Box**
>
> **unsafe**—dangerous
> **unlucky**—having bad luck
> **unhurt**—safe
> **untrue**—false
> **unfinished**—not done
> **unafraid**—not scared

1. "I lost my lunch money. My homework paper tore. I was late for school," said Bobby. "This has been an _____ day."
2. It is _____ to cross the street against the light.
3. Robin couldn't go out to play because her seatwork was

   _____ .
4. The story Jerry told about finding a dinosaur egg was

   _____ .
5. Yesterday Connie fell out of the apple tree. Thank goodness she was _____
6. Julio was _____ as he came close to the haunted house.

Learn About

The Prefix im-

One more prefix is *im-*. The prefix *im-* also means "not."

Example

Mature means "grown-up."
Immature means "not grown-up."
Larry is so immature that he's no fun to play with.

Activity 2

In my Word Box are words with the prefix *im-*. Read the words and their meanings. Next read the sentences below the Word Box. Then finish each sentence with a **boldfaced** word from the Word Box.

> **Word Box**
>
> **impossible**—not likely to happen
> **impatient**—restless and fidgety
> **improper**—not proper or correct
> **impolite**—rude
> **impure**—not clean

1. Dad was late. Mom became _____ waiting for him.
2. Children who eat with their fingers are using _____ table manners.
3. The water in the brook tastes funny. Our teacher says it must be _____ .

4. Barry tried to lift his dad off the floor. Everyone thought that was an _____ task.
5. Cindy stepped on Carl's toe. She didn't say excuse me. Cindy was being very _____ .

Activity 3

Now find and circle each word you learned in **Activity 2** and the following words in the Word Search puzzle: *unsafe, unlucky, unhurt, untrue, unfinished, unafraid*. The words go across and down. One is done for you.

```
X Y Z I M P O S S I B L E
A B C M D E U F F M G H I
P Q R P S S N I M P U R E
U N S A F E L M A O B C C
N W X T Y Z U P Q L E E D
A H J I K L C R M I M S S
F Z Z E Q Q K O V T V L L
R P Q N R R Y P L E W V V
A U N T R U E E L Q S S Z
I W X U N H U R T Q A B C
D X U N F I N I S H E D Z
```

> **Jack-in-the-Box's rule number 5 for learning words:** Learn the meaning of *un-* and *im-*. Remember how *un-* and *im-* change word meanings.

15

Prefix
Crossword Puzzle Number 2

Activity 4

Look at the words in the Word Box. They are words you have learned with the prefixes *un-* and *im-*.

Now read the word meanings beside the crossword puzzle. Then choose a word from the Word Box that goes with each meaning. Write the word in the puzzle. Be sure to follow the numbers across and down. The letters in the puzzle will help you.

Word Box

unsafe, unhurt, unlucky, untrue, unfinished, unafraid, impossible, impatient, impure, impolite, improper

Across
2. false
3. not done
5. rude
6. restless and fidgety
7. having bad luck
8. dangerous

Down
1. not clean
2. not scared
4. not likely to happen
6. not proper or correct
7. safe

Show All You Know

About Prefixes

Draw lines to match each word below with its meaning.

dishonest   come into sight again

reappear   restless

unsafe   not truthful

impatient   dangerous

untrue   not clean

impure   false

retrace   mess

disorder   go over lines on a paper again

Choose words from the Word Box to finish each sentence below.

Word Box
replaced, refill, unafraid, impolite, unhurt, impossible, disagree, dislikes

1. Carmen _____ green beans.
2. On our trip we had to _____ the car's gas tank three times.
3. Debbie was _____ of the dentist.
4. Pedro thought getting all A's on his report card was _____ .
5. Joe fell off his bike but was _____ .

6. Annie never says thank you. She is so _____ .
7. Charlie _____ his fishbowl with a new fish tank.
8. Karen and Grace always _____ about which TV show to watch.

Read each meaning below. Write the word that matches it on the line. The first one is done for you.

1. not to go on doing something
   _____ discontinue _____
2. open again _____
3. not to like something _____
4. having bad luck _____
5. not proper or correct _____
6. not afraid _____
7. fill again _____
8. not honest _____
9. safe _____

Now find and circle the matching words in the puzzle.

```
N U N A F R A I D U A
X I M P R O P E R N B
O U N H U R T K S L R
D I S C O N T I N U E
P Q R S P T U S V C O
F G H R E F I L L K P
D I S L I K E I W Y E
R D I S H O N E S T N
```

Learn About

Suffixes

You have already learned what a prefix is

(1) a group of letters

(2) added to the beginning of a word

(3) to change the word's meaning.

Now you are ready to learn what a *suffix* (SUHF-iks) is.

1. A suffix is also a group of letters that has its own meaning.
   - *-Er* is a suffix. *-Er* means "a person who."

2. A suffix is added to the **end** of a word.
   - teach + er = teacher

3. A suffix changes the meaning of a word.
   - *Teach* means "to help someone learn." A *teacher* is "a person who teaches, or helps someone learn."

Activity 1

Look at the words in the Word Box. Then study each picture. Figure out the kind of work each person does. Write your answer on the line nearest each picture.

Word Box
builder, painter, trainer, dancer, driver

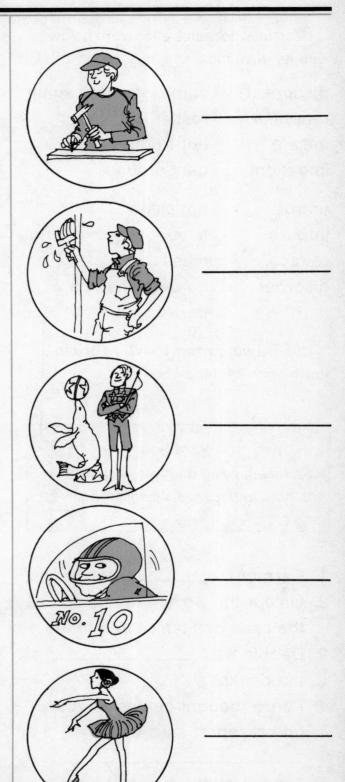

Learn About

The Suffix -ful

Another suffix is -ful. -Ful means "filled with."

Example

Wonder means "a feeling of surprise."
Wonderful means "filled with surprise or wonder."
The circus was wonderful.

Activity 2

All the words in the Word Box end with the suffix -ful. First study the words. Next read each paragraph. Then finish each paragraph with a word from the Word Box.

Word Box
harmful, colorful, wasteful, careful, cheerful

1. Juan has a cheery smile. He is always happy. Juan is a _____ boy.

2. Most snakes cause no harm. But others give off a poison when they bite. Learn the kinds of snakes that can be _____ .

3. Gina plays with many toys. She takes good care of them. Gina is very _____ about putting them away in her toy box.

4. Al never finishes his lunch. He wastes a lot of food. Throwing away good food is _____ .

5. Mary's painting was very bright. She used many colors. Mary painted a _____ picture.

Activity 3

Write the correct -ful word for each meaning below.

1. filled with wonder _____
2. filled with cheer _____
3. filled with harm _____
4. filled with care _____
5. filled with waste _____

Jack-in-the-Box's rule number 6 for learning words: Learn the meanings of -er and -ful. Remember how -er and -ful change word meanings.

Suffix
Crossword Puzzle Number 1

Activity 4

Read the word meanings below the crossword puzzle. Next think of a word you have learned that goes with each meaning. Then write each word in the puzzle. Be sure to follow the numbers across and down. The letters in the puzzle will help you.

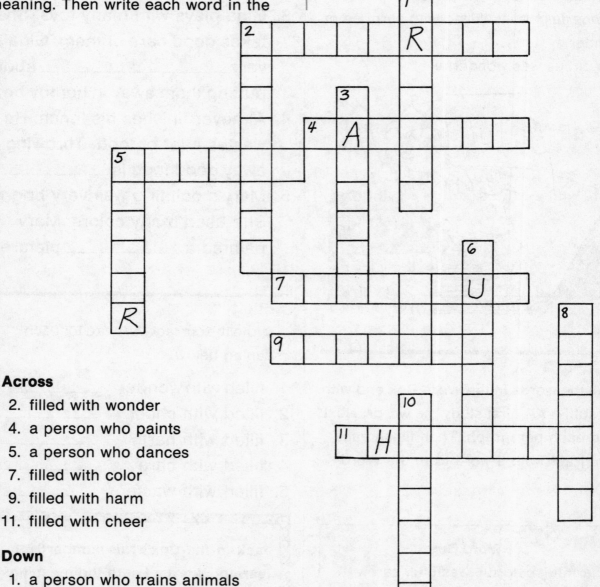

Across

2. filled with wonder
4. a person who paints
5. a person who dances
7. filled with color
9. filled with harm
11. filled with cheer

Down

1. a person who trains animals
2. filled with waste
3. filled with care
5. a person who drives
6. a person who builds
8. a person who works with jewels
10. a person who teaches

Learn About

The Suffix -less

Another suffix that pops up a lot is -less. -Less means "without."

Example

Fearless means "without fear."
Everyone cheered when the fearless skier made her jump.

Activity 1

All the words in the Word Box end with the suffix -less. First study the words. Next read each paragraph. Then finish each story with a word from the Word Box.

Word Box

endless, homeless, thoughtless, noiseless, careless, helpless, friendless, nameless

1. Lisa is often mean to people. That's why she doesn't have any friends to play with. Lisa is
_____ .

2. Ray rides his bike in the middle of the road. He doesn't take care to look both ways before crossing streets. Someday Ray may be sorry for his _____ ways.

3. Tabby's kittens are so tiny. They must be washed and fed by their mother. They can't do anything without help from Tabby. Until they get bigger, Tabby's kittens are _____ .

4. After the fire, the Smith family had no home to live in. They were _____ .

5. Brenda got a puppy for her birthday. She couldn't think of a name for the puppy. So the puppy went _____ .

6. At one time trains made a lot of noise. Many changes were made. Now trains are almost _____ .

7. The movie was very long. Brent felt it would never end. He thought the movie seemed
_____ .

8. Fred never says thank you. His thoughts are never of anyone's feelings, either. Fred is a
_____ boy.

Now write a meaning for each word in the Word Box.

endless _____

thoughtless _____

noiseless _____

careless _____

friendless _____

helpless _____

nameless _____

homeless _____

Learn About

The Suffix -ness

The last suffix that pops out of my Word Box is *-ness. -Ness* means "the state or act of being."

Example

Kindness means "the act of being kind." After the party the children thanked Mrs. Gomez for her kindness.

Activity 2

In each sentence that follows there is a word with the suffix *-ness.* Read the sentences. Next read the three choices of words below each sentence. Then underline the correct meaning of the **boldfaced** word in each sentence.

1. The movie house suddenly went from bright lights to **darkness.**

   nighttime   no lights   daytime

2. The **suddenness** of the snowstorm caused a traffic jam.

   warning   surprise
              quick happening

3. Mother was surprised by the **neatness** of Jane's bedroom.

   order   strength   wonder

4. After the ball game Nancy felt a **weakness** in her pitching arm.

   pain   lack of strength   danger

5. The **sweetness** of the candy made everyone ask for another piece.

   good taste   good time   good day

Activity 3

Write a meaning for each word below. Remember *-ness* means "the state or act of being."

1. slowness _____

   _____

2. closeness _____

   _____

3. shortness _____

   _____

4. happiness* _____

   _____

5. ugliness* _____

   _____

6. loneliness* _____

   _____

* In words ending with *y*, change the *y* to *i* before adding *-ness*.

> **Jack-in-the-Box's rule number 7 for learning words:** Learn the meaning of *-less* and *-ness*. Remember how *-less* and *-ness* change word meanings.

Suffix
Crossword Puzzle Number 2

Activity 4

Look at the words in the Word Box. They are words you have learned with the suffixes *-less* and *-ness.*

Read the word meanings beside the crossword puzzle. Then choose a word from the Word Box that goes with each meaning. Write the word in the puzzle. Be sure to follow the numbers across and down. The letters in the puzzle will help you.

Word Box

suddenness, endless, careless, friendless, nameless, sweetness, neatness, thoughtless, homeless, helpless, darkness, noiseless, weakness

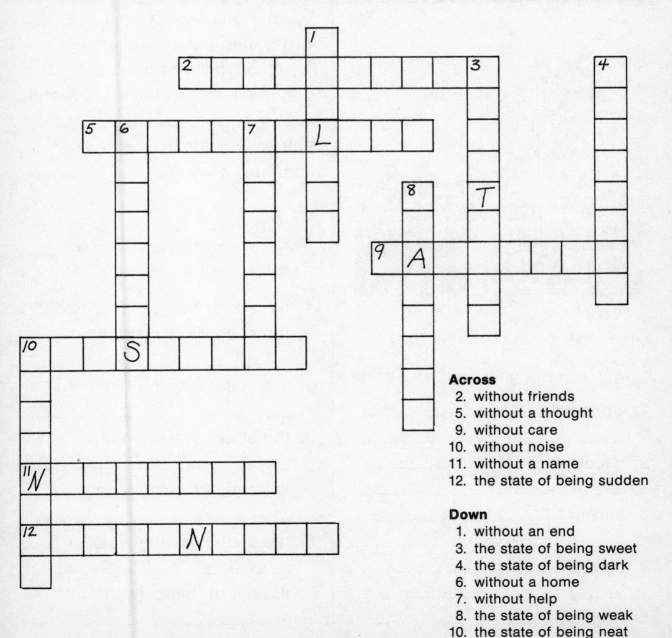

Across
2. without friends
5. without a thought
9. without care
10. without noise
11. without a name
12. the state of being sudden

Down
1. without an end
3. the state of being sweet
4. the state of being dark
6. without a home
7. without help
8. the state of being weak
10. the state of being neat

23

Show All You Know

About Suffixes

Write a word that matches each meaning below. One is done for you.

1. a person who dances <u>dancer</u>
2. a person who builds _____
3. a person who paints _____
4. a person who teaches _____
5. a person who trains _____
6. a person who drives _____

Write a meaning for each word below.

1. wonderful _____

_____

2. cheerful _____

_____

3. harmful _____

_____

4. careful _____

_____

5. colorful _____

Finish each sentence with a word ending with the suffix *-less.*

1. If a puppy has no home, it is

_____ .

2. If a road is so long it seems like it will never end, the road is _____ .

3. If a boy doesn't care how he writes his papers, he is _____

4. If a man can't do anything without help, he is _____ .

5. If a girl doesn't have any friends, she is _____ .

6. If your goldfish don't have names, they are _____ .

Write a word that matches each meaning. The first one is done for you.

1. the act of being kind <u>kindness</u>
2. the state of being slow

_____

3. the state of being happy

_____

4. the state of being neat

_____

5. the state of being lonely

_____

6. the state of being weak

_____

7. the act of being sweet

Learn About
Word Clues

Pop up and give yourself another cheer for having learned about suffixes. Now get ready to find another way to learn new words.

Suppose you don't know a word meaning. Sometimes the meaning is hidden in the sentence or paragraph. Words that come before or after the unknown word or words may help you figure out meanings.

Keep your eyes open for hidden meanings of words you don't know.

Activity 1

Read the story. Follow the directions after the story.

Mother Rabbit's Trick

One day Mother Rabbit took Little Rabbit into the woods.

"You must learn what is edible," said Mother Rabbit to Little Rabbit. "*Edible* means 'things you can eat.'"

Little Rabbit pointed to a rock.

"Can I eat that?" he asked.

"No," said Mother Rabbit. "A rock is not edible."

A little gray mouse hopped by.

"Can I eat the mouse?" asked Little Rabbit.

"No," said Mother Rabbit. "We rabbits are *vegetarians* [vej-ə-TAIR-ee-ən]. Vegetarians eat only plants."

Suddenly a big hawk flew over their heads.

"Run," cried Mother Rabbit. Then she dived into a hole. But Hawk had trapped Little Rabbit behind a tree.

"I'm going to eat you," said Hawk.

"Oh, don't eat him," shouted Mother Rabbit. "He's not a real rabbit."

"What is he?" asked Hawk.

"A gingerbread rabbit," she said.

"What's gingerbread?" asked Hawk.

"*Gingerbread* is a cake made from flour and a spice called ginger," answered Mother Rabbit.

"Flour? Yuck!" said Hawk, and he flew away.

"My trick worked," said Mother Rabbit. Then she and Little Rabbit began to laugh.

Now underline the meaning of each word below in the story. Then write each meaning on the lines.

1. edible _____
   _____

2. vegetarians _____
   _____

3. gingerbread _____
   _____

Jack-in-the-Box's rule number 8 for learning words: Look for meanings of unknown words in the words before and after them.

Learn More

About Word Clues

Read the story about Betsy's visitor from England—a country across the ocean from the United States.

Baseball Game

"Let's watch TV," said Betsy.

"TV?" asked Meg. "What's that?"

"TV is television," said Betsy.

"Oh!" laughed Meg. "In England we call it the telly."

Betsy turned on the TV. A baseball game was on.

"It's the last of the ninth," the sports announcer said.

"Baseball games have parts called innings," said Betsy.

"George Brown is at the plate," said the announcer.

"He's talking about home plate," said Betsy. "The batter stands at the plate. The pitcher throws the ball to the batter. If the

batter hits it, he runs. He tries to get all the way around the three bases and back to home plate. If he does, he scores a run."

". . . And Brown hits a fly ball," said the announcer.

"A fly ball is a ball that is hit into the air," said Betsy. "That one looks easy to catch."

Just then a player caught the fly ball. George Brown was out.

"Well," said Meg, "I guess you called that play. Baseball looks like a jolly good game!"

"Jolly good?" asked Betsy with a puzzled look on her face.

Find a word or words in the story that go with each meaning. Write the words on the lines.

1. another word for TV _____
2. what the parts of a baseball game are called _____
3. the player who throws the ball

   _____
4. the player who tries to hit the ball _____
5. where the batter stands

   _____
6. what the batter scores if he runs around three bases and back to home plate_____
7. a ball hit into the air

   _____

Practice Finding
Word Clues

Activity 3

Read the story.

Cloud Talk

Have you ever tried to read the sky? You can learn how to very easily.

A very tall cloud is called a *thunderhead*. The top of the cloud may be 5 miles high. This cloud brings thunderstorms, snow, and hail. Lightning often flashes inside a thunderhead.

When the sun shines brightly, the air near the Earth is warmed. This warm air forms an air bubble and starts to rise. The water in the bubble turns into tiny drops. These drops form into *cumulus* (KYOOM-yə-ləss) clouds. Cumulus clouds are white and fluffy. They look like cotton. Cumulus clouds mean the weather will be fair.

Clouds that form 7 or 8 miles above the Earth are called *cirrus* (SIHR-əss). Cirrus clouds look like curls of smoke. They are made up of bits of ice. Cirrus clouds tell you a storm may be on its way.

Go outside and study the clouds. What do you see? What kind of weather will there be?

Now find a word in the story that goes with each meaning below.

1. a cloud made of bits of ice

   _____

2. a cloud that is about 5 miles high _____

3. a cloud that looks like cotton

   _____

4. a cloud that brings thunderstorms

   _____

5. a cloud that tells you a storm may be on its way _____

6. a cloud that means fair weather

   _____

Activity 4

Below are words you have learned. Number each list in ABC (alphabetical) order.

A		B	
vegetarian	___	gingerbread	___
fly ball	___	pitcher	___
innings	___	television	___
batter	___	home plate	___
run	___	cumulus	

Show All You Know

About Word Clues

Underline the best meaning for each **boldfaced** word below.

1. **edible**
   a. sweet-tasting
   b. safe to eat

2. **vegetarian**
   a. animal that doesn't eat vegetables
   b. animal that eats only plants

3. **pitcher**
   a. the player who throws the ball to the batter
   b. the player who hits the ball

4. **fly ball**
   a. a ball hit on the ground
   b. a ball hit into the air

5. **cirrus**
   a. a cloud made up of bits of ice
   b. a cloud that is about 5 miles high

6. **cumulus**
   a. a cloud that means fair weather
   b. a cloud made up of bits of ice

Practice finding word clues in the story that follows. Study the picture. Read the story. Follow the directions after the story.

A Special Kind of Machine

What is a *robot* (ROH-bət)?

A robot is a machine. But it is a special kind of machine.

Most machines need a person around in order to work. But a robot doesn't. Once a robot is started, it does a job automatically—without a person's help.

In the future there may be many robots around. Robots might do surprising things for you. They may even do your homework!

Write a meaning for *robot*.

_____

_____

Write a meaning for *automatically*.

_____

_____

Learn About Words

With Multiple Meanings

Many words in my Word Box have multiple (MUHL-tə-pəl) meanings. *Multiple* means "more than one." So, words with multiple meanings have more than one meaning.

Example

Fido made paw **prints** in the mud.
Carmela **prints** her name neatly.

Activity 1

Study each picture and read each word meaning.

A **train** is a line of railroad cars. You can **train** a dog to sit up and beg for food.

Flowers grow in the **spring.** You can **spring** out of bed.

A pilot can **land** a plane. A farm may have a lot of **land** for planting crops.

A **cook** makes a meal. Your dad can **cook** hamburgers.

Now finish each sentence below with a **boldfaced** word.

1. On our trip we traveled over _____ and across the sea.
2. On my birthday Mom will _____ my favorite meal.
3. Grandpa took us on a _____ ride to the big city.
4. Birds build their nests in the _____ .
5. We watched a helicopter _____ on the roof of a tall building.
6. Matthew says he can _____ his puppy to roll over.
7. The _____ served us eggs.
8. I turn off the alarm clock and _____ out of bed.

Jack-in-the-Box's rule number 9 for learning words: For each word you learn, try to think if the word has more than one meaning.

Learn More Words
With Multiple Meanings

Activity 2

In the sentences below there are words with multiple meanings. Read the sentences. Read the words below each sentence. Then underline the meaning for the **boldfaced** word in each sentence.

1. The children rode the bus to **school.**

   a place where students learn

   a large number of fish

2. Through the glass-bottomed boat we could see a **school** of fish.

   a place where students learn

   a large number of fish

3. Mother served the cake on her new **plate.**

   the home base in baseball

   a flat dish for food

4. Jodi threw the ball to the **plate.**

   the home base in baseball

   a flat dish for food

5. It took a **lot** of paint to finish the poster.

   a large amount   a piece of land

6. The kids played ball in the empty **lot.**

   a large amount   a piece of land

7. Dad gave Mom a pretty **ring.**

   the sound of a bell

   something worn on the finger

8. The **ring** of the telephone woke me up.

   the sound of a bell

   something worn on the finger

9. We climbed to the **top** of the hill.

   a cover   the highest part

10. Mom put the **top** on the jelly jar.

    a cover   the highest part

Activity 3

The words below are from the last two lessons. Number each list of words in ABC (alphabetical) order.

	A			B	
ring	_____		train	_____
spring	_____		school	_____
plate	_____		cook	_____
prints	_____		plane	_____
lot	_____		top	_____

Using a
Dictionary

Sometimes you can't figure out the meaning of an unknown word from the words that come before or after it. Then you should look up the word in a dictionary.

You have already had some practice listing words in ABC (alphabetical) order. Words in a dictionary are listed in ABC order too. First find the word. Then read all the meanings for that word. Decide which meaning fits the word as it is used in the sentence you just read.

Activity 4

Below is part of a dictionary page. Study the page.

hive	**1.** A box or container built for bees to live in. **2.** A large number of bees that live together.
hobby	An occupation that you enjoy doing apart from your usual studies or work; something done for fun. Cooking is my father's *hobby.*
hockey	A game played on ice or on a field by players who move a ball or flat object with long sticks. Players in ice *hockey* wear skates.
hoe	A garden tool with a small blade and a long handle. A *hoe* is used for digging in soil.
hog	**1.** A pig, especially a large one. **2.** A greedy or selfish person.

Now finish each sentence with a word from the sample dictionary page. If a word has two meanings, write the number of the meaning you chose in the box at the end of the sentence. The first one is done for you.

1. Farmer Gray feeds his __hog__ corncobs and potato peels. ☐1

2. Grandpa loosened the soil with a _____ . ☐

3. Bruce was stung when he stepped on a _____ of bees. ☐

4. Jennifer's _____ is sewing. ☐

5. The _____ team skated onto the ice. ☐

6. Sometimes Pete eats like a _____ . ☐

7. Martie wanted to raise bees, so Dad built her a _____ . ☐

Show All You Know
About Words With Multiple Meanings

Draw lines to match each word to its meaning.

school   leap

spring   a group of fish

land   bake

cook   soil

train   a time of year

spring   chef

land   locomotive

cook   set down an airplane

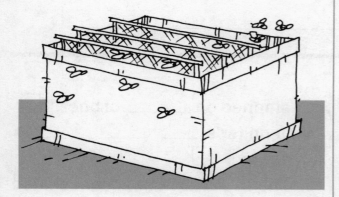

plate   a piece of land

lot   flat dish

hive   something done for fun

hobby   a box for bees to live in

ring   sound of a bell

List the words below in the order they would be found in a dictionary.

hoe _____

top _____

school _____

hog _____

lot _____

Write one meaning for the word *school.*

1. _____

_____

Write a sentence for that meaning of *school.*

1. _____

_____

Write one meaning for *ring.*

1. _____

_____

Write a sentence for that meaning of *ring.*

1. _____

_____

Write one meaning for *hog.*

1. _____

_____

Write a sentence for that meaning of *hog.*

1. _____

_____

Learn About
Compound Words

Two words are sometimes joined together to make a new word. The new word is called a *compound word.*

Example: flower + pot = flowerpot

If you come across a compound word you don't know the meaning of, ask yourself these questions:

- What two words make up the compound word?
- Do I know the meaning of one or both words?
- Do the words before or after the unknown word give me a clue to its meaning?

Activity 1

Read the words in my Word Box. Then join each word to a word in the list below the Word Box to make a compound word. Write the two words as one.

> **Word Box**
> saw, glasses, corn, crow, teller, case, ground, card

1. play _____
2. see _____
3. pop _____
4. suit _____
5. eye _____
6. story _____
7. post _____
8. scare _____

Now finish each sentence below with a compound word you have made.

1. The farmer put a _____ in the cornfield.
2. Jan couldn't see the chalkboard because she wasn't wearing her _____ .
3. The class races were held on the _____ .
4. The _____ worked puppets as she told the story.
5. Jean sat on one end of the _____ and Joan sat on the other.
6. During the movie we ate two boxes of _____ .
7. On his vacation John sent us a _____ .
8. After Sue finished packing her _____ , she left for camp.

> **Jack-in-the-Box's rule number 10 for learning words:** Use words you know to make as many compound words as you can.

33

Learn More
Compound Words

Activity 2

Read the words in my Word Box. Next read each clue. Find a compound word from the Word Box that matches each meaning. Write each word on the chain puzzle. The **last** letter of each word is also the **first** letter of the next word. The first one is done for you.

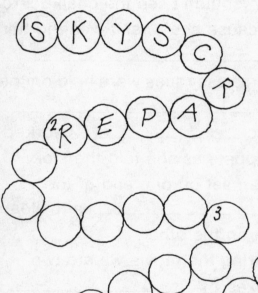

Word Box

goldfish, tablecloth, headache, skyscraper, keyhole, homework, raincoat, earring

Clues

1. A tall building
2. A coat worn when it rains
3. Material used to cover a table
4. A pain in the head
5. Something worn on the ear
6. A small fish
7. Schoolwork done at home
8. An opening into which a key fits

Activity 3

Write a sentence using each compound word below.

1. flashlight _____

_____

2. haircut _____

_____

3. airplane _____

_____

Compound Word
Crossword Puzzle

Activity 4

Read the word meanings beside the crossword puzzle. Then choose a compound word from the Word Box for each meaning. Write the compound words in the puzzle. Be sure to follow the numbers across and down. The letters in the puzzle will help you.

Word Box

headlight, sailboat, grapefruit, lifeboat, playroom, football, iceberg, rainbow, goldenrod, handbag, daylight, firewood, outdoors, railroad

Across

1. a boat used to save people on a sinking ship
4. a curve of colors seen in the sky after a rain shower
6. a wild plant with small yellow flowers and a long stem
8. a small pocketbook
9. wood for a stove or fireplace
11. light from the sun
13. a boat that is moved by the wind
14. something to help drivers see at night

Down

2. a large chunk of ice floating in the ocean
3. a room used for fun and games
5. a game in which players pass, kick, and run with a ball
7. in the open air
10. the tracks a train runs on
12. something to eat that is round and yellow

35

Show All You Know

About Compound Words

Draw lines to match the first part of the compound word to the second part.

see	saw
pop	case
scare	corn
suit	crow
play	ground

gold	scraper
sky	cloth
rain	fish
home	coat
table	work

eye	ache
story	glasses
post	teller
head	card
ear	ring

key	rod
golden	hole
day	ball
life	light
foot	boat

Finish each sentence in the next column with a word from the Word Box.

Word Box

headlight, outdoors, sailboat, firewood, grapefruit, handbag, playroom, iceberg

1. The _____ on Mom's car burned out.
2. The wind moved the _____ over the waves.
3. For breakfast I ate a juicy _____.
4. We held the birthday party in the _____.
5. The huge ship almost struck the _____.
6. Mom put her car keys into her _____.
7. We gathered _____ for the campfire.
8. The wagon was left _____ in the rain.

Learn Words
From Stories

I've pulled some stories out of my Word Box for you to read. All the stories contain words you have learned or whose meanings you can figure out. Let's begin with a story about monsters!

Activity 1

Read the story.

Who Is the Monster?

One sunny day Peter Porcupine walked in the woods. Peter was happy. He hummed a happy **tune.**

Suddenly Peter stopped humming. He saw a strange **creature.** Peter ran home.

"Mother!" shouted Peter. "I saw a monster come out from behind a **thicket.**"

"A monster?" said Mother. "What did it look like?"

"It was made of stone," said Peter. "It had a head and four legs. It crawled. It was **horrible.**"

"We will go to the woods," said Mother. "I want to see this monster."

On that same day Tom Turtle had walked in the woods. Tom was happy. He hummed a happy tune.

Suddenly Tom stopped humming. He saw a strange creature. He **dashed** home.

"Mother!" shouted Tom. "I saw a monster in the woods."

"A monster?" said Mother. "What did it look like?"

"It was fat. It had pins all over its body. It was horrible," said Tom.

"We will go to the woods," said Mother. "I want to see the monster."

Finally, the two turtles and the two porcupines met in the woods. Both young animals came face-to-face with their monsters. Mother Turtle and Mother Porcupine laughed.

"You **foolish** children," said Mother Turtle. "Neither of you is a monster. You are both animals."

"You should be friends," said Mother Porcupine. "Now run along and play."

And that's just what Peter and Tom did.

Now write a **boldfaced** word from the story next to each meaning below.

1. a thick clump of bushes _____
2. a song _____
3. raced _____
4. silly _____
5. awful _____
6. an animal _____

> **Jack-in-the-Box's rule number 11 for learning words:** When reading stories, first try to figure out the meanings of unknown words. Then look up those words in a dictionary to make sure you are right.

Learn Words
From Poems

Activity 2

Read the poem.

Bradford's Adventure

Bradford the tiger
Awoke one fine day,
Got out of bed,
And went out to play.

Off through the **jungle**
That grew all around,
Brad went with his nose
Sniff-sniffing the ground.

He'd gone pretty far
Just **loping** along,
When Brad had a thought
That something was wrong.

For nowhere around
Could Brad hear a sound!
And nowhere in sight
Were animals found!

"That's so **peculiar**,"
Said Brad. "Let me think."
He stopped by the lake
To get a cool drink.

Then without warning,
Brad saw a **huge** man,
Brad turned in a flash!
Like lightning he ran.

He ran and he ran
Till breath seemed all gone,
But he didn't stop . . .
He just **scurried** on.

Till safe in his **lair**
He **leaped** into bed.
Thoughts of the **peril**
Were fresh in his head.

So Brad made a rule
And follows it still,
"I'll not go alone
Nor far from this hill.

"I'd rather stay here
With friends that I've got.
Look for adventure?
Who me? I need not!"

Now write a **boldfaced** word from the story next to each meaning below.

1. to run, taking long steps _____
2. the living place of a wild animal

   _____

3. land thickly covered with trees
   and plants _____
4. odd or strange _____
5. very big _____
6. jumped _____
7. danger _____
8. ran quickly _____

Learn More Words
From Stories

Activity 3

Read the story.

The Lost Button

"What are you looking for?" Andy asked Rob.

Rob ran his fingers through the **damp** grass. He felt something round. He picked it up. It was just an old bottle cap. He **tossed** it away.

"I'm looking for a button," Rob **whispered.**

"Is it a **valuable** button?" Andy asked, whispering back.

"Yes," Rob whispered.

"Is it a magic button?" whispered Andy. "Or part of some treasure?"

"Don't be silly," Rob whispered.

"Why do you have to find it?" Andy whispered.

"Because it fell off my new jacket," Rob whispered.

Andy sat back on the grass. He looked at his friend. "Is that all?" he whispered. "Then what's the big secret?"

Rob shook his head. "It isn't a big secret," he whispered.

Andy was **confused.** "Then why are we whispering to each other?" he asked.

Rob started laughing. "I don't know about you, but I'm whispering because I can't talk," he said. "I have a bad cold!"

Now write a **boldfaced** word from the story next to each meaning below.

1. threw _____
2. mixed-up _____
3. worth a great deal of money

   _____

4. spoke softly _____
5. slightly wet _____

Activity 4

Number each list of words in alphabetical order.

A		B	
valuable	____	peculiar	____
whispered	____	lair	____
tossed	____	scurried	____
damp	____	jungle	____
confused	____	leaped	____

Show All You Know
About Learning Words from Stories

Below are meanings of words you have learned. Write a word from the Word Box that matches each meaning. Then find and circle each word in the puzzle.

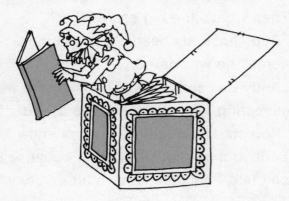

Word Box
confused, scurried, huge, peculiar, loping, foolish, tune, damp, dashed, whispered, thicket, valuable, peril, horrible, leaped, creature, jungle, lair, tossed

1. a song _____
2. raced _____
3. a thick clump of bushes
   _____
4. awful _____
5. an animal _____
6. the living place of a wild animal
   _____
7. land thickly covered with trees and plants _____
8. jumped _____
9. danger _____
10. threw _____

11. worth a great deal of money
    _____
12. spoke softly _____
13. slightly wet _____

```
V X T H I C K E T Y
A Z L E A P E D U W
L A B C C D D E N H
U H O R R I B L E I
A O W P E R I L V S
B S S D A S H E D P
L S Q Q T R R V L E
E Z P J U N G L E R
W L A I R D A M P E
T O S S E D L O M D
```

Now finish each sentence below with a word from the Word Box. **Hint:** Use the words not found in the Word Search puzzle.

1. It is _____ to think cows can fly.
2. The campers snapped pictures of deer _____ across the open field.
3. The clown was dressed in a _____ outfit.
4. Tammy's birthday gift was in a _____ package.
5. The squirrel gathered some nuts, then _____ up a tree.
6. Bruce became _____ when he lost his way.

Learn About
Homophones

Sometimes two words sound the same. But they are not spelled the same, and they have different meanings. These words are called *homophones*.

Activity 1

Study the pictures and the **boldfaced** words below the pictures. Then finish each sentence with a **boldfaced** word.

dough   **doe**

pain   **pane**

1. Pete's fly ball broke the _____ in Mr. Garcia's window.
2. The _____ and her fawn drank water from the lake.
3. Grandma put the bread _____ into the oven.
4. The _____ of his broken arm made David cry.

Activity 2

Below are more sentences with homophones. Read each sentence.

You carry sand or water in a **pail.**
If you are sick, your face may look **pale.**
You can dig up the **root** of a plant.
Your **route** to school goes through the park.

Now finish each sentence with a **boldfaced** word from above.

1. We followed a _____ that took us over the mountains.
2. We carried the fish we caught in a large _____ .
3. Dad thought I looked a little _____ , so he took my temperature.
4. The _____ of a plant soaks up water from the soil.

Jack-in-the-Box's rule number 12 for learning words: For each word you learn, try to think if the word has a homophone.

Learn More

About Homophones

Activity 3

Finish each sentence with a homophone from the Word Box. Then write each word in the crossword puzzle. Be sure to follow the numbers across and down. The letters in the puzzle will help you.

Word Box

break, brake, beet, beat, aloud, allowed, peace, piece, cent, scent

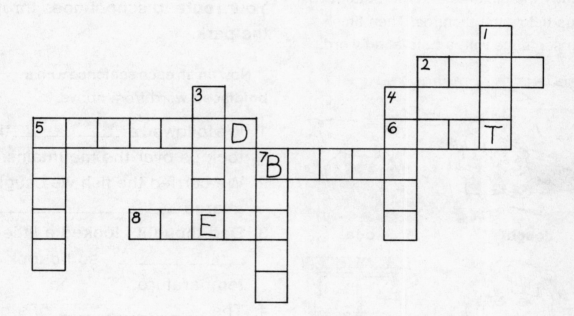

Across

2. The farmer pulled a _____ from his garden.
5. Mother _____ us to go ice-skating.
6. I don't have one _____ to spend.
7. Dad stopped the car by putting on the hand _____ .
8. Susie ate the last _____ of cake.

Down

1. Dad let me _____ the cream for the cake.
3. Everyone wants _____ in the world.
4. Skunks have a strong _____ .
5. Fred laughed _____ at the funny joke.
7. Oh, no! Did Mom _____ another dish?

Learn About
Homographs

Now that you know about homophones, let's meet *homographs.*

Sometimes two words are spelled the same but don't sound the same. They don't have the same meaning either. These words are called *homographs.*

The word *close* is a homograph. *Close* (KLOHSS) means "nearby." *Close* (KLOHZ) means "to shut."

Activity 4

In each sentence below there is a homograph. Read the sentences. Be sure to pronounce each homograph correctly.

1. Sally wears a **bow** (BOH) in her hair. After the play, the star took a **bow** (BOW).
2. A **dove** (DUHV) can build a nest in the fir tree. Everyone clapped as Cindy **dove** (DOHV) into the swimming pool.
3. I **live** (LIV) in New York. Jerry's pet is a **live** (LIGHV) snake.
4. Aaron tries to **read** (REED) every day. Last week he **read** (RED) five books.

Now finish each sentence below with a homograph from Activity 4.

1. Penny put a big red _____ on the package.
2. Yesterday I _____ a good story.
3. The _____ flew into the air.
4. Carlos _____ into the pool and came up with a penny.
5. What story will the teacher _____ next?
6. After her song, the singer took a _____ .
7. Where do you _____ ?
8. My sister pretends that her teddy bear is a _____ bear.

> **Jack-in-the-Box's rule number 13 for learning words:** For each word you learn, try to think if the word has a homograph.

43

Show All You Know

About Homophones and Homographs

Underline the correct *homophone* for each sentence below.

1. The (doe, dough) darted across the open field.
2. Dad makes (doe, dough) out of flour and water.
3. The medicine helped Mom's (pain, pane) go away.
4. The (pain, pane) in the window was cracked.
5. The Tigers football team (beat, beet) the Lions, 12 to 6.
6. Grandma put a huge (beat, beet) in her soup.
7. The teacher read the story (allowed, aloud).
8. We are not (allowed, aloud) to go swimming after supper.
9. Lee ate the last (peace, piece) of cake.
10. The teacher wanted some (peace, piece) and quiet in the room.
11. We knew where the fox was hiding by its (scent, cent).
12. Lisa found 1 (scent, cent) on the bus.
13. To stop the car, Mom pulled the hand (brake, break).
14. Did your little sister (brake, break) my balloon?

Nice going, vocabulary wizard.

Underline the correct meaning for the *homograph* in each sentence below.

1. Sarah tied a **bow** in her hair.
   a. the shape of a ribbon tied into loops
   b. to bend from the waist as a sign of thanks
2. The **dove** pecked at the bread.
   a. went into the water headfirst
   b. a kind of bird
3. There are many **live** animals in the zoo.
   a. not dead
   b. to have a home
4. Dad wants to **read** the newspaper.
   a. to look at and speak aloud
   b. to look at and understand written words

My Word List

Answers

P. 1. lots, peek, dwell, too, Girls and Boys. **P. 2.** 1. woods, 2. afraid, 3. wise, 4. pretty, 5. large, 6. town, 7. field, 8. great, 9. bandit, 10. wagon. **P. 3.** Across—3. children, 5. terrific, 8. huge, 11. field, 13. bandit, 14. town, Down—1. scared, 2. beautiful, 4. dwell, 6. forest, 7. clever, 9. many, 10. peek, 12. also, 15. wagon. **P. 4.** 1. merry, 2. warm, 3. empty, 4. sad, 5. wealthy, 6. full, 7. cool, 8. poor. **P. 5.** 1. not curved, 2. without strength, 3. close together, 4. not beautiful, 5. to finish; weak. **P. 6.** Across—3. merry, 4. warm, 5. wealthy, 9. straight, Down—1. narrow, 2. start, 6. empty, 7. ugly, 8. strong; 1. wealthy, 2. merry, 3. warm, 4. narrow, 5. empty. **P. 7.** Answers may vary. 1. tame, 2. terrific, 3. gigantic, 4. smile, 5. awful, 6. tiny, 7. wild, 8. grin. **P. 8.** 1. repair, 2. cry, 3. bottom, 4. ill, 5. hello, 6. healthy, 7. sob, 8. good-bye, 9. peak, 10. break. **P. 9.** 2. wild, 3. awful, 4. small, 5. frown, 6. top, 7. repair, 8. cry, 9. healthy, 10. farewell, 11. hello, 12. bottom. **P. 10.** peek—look, dwell—live, scared—afraid, town—village, beautiful—pretty, forest—woods, too—also, thief—robber, wise—clever, wagon—cart. 1. field, 2. tiny, 3. wild, 4. terrible, 5. smile, begin—complete, empty—full, wealthy—poor, warm—cool, crooked—straight, smile—frown, ugly—pretty, strong—weak. 1. gigantic, 2. narrow, 3. tame, 4. frown. **P. 11.** 2. dishonest—not truthful, 3. disorder—not neat, 4. disagree—not to think the same, 5. dislike—not to care for something. 1. disorder, 2. dislikes, 3. disagree, 4. dishonest. **P. 12.** 1. refilled, 2. replaced, 3. reopen, 4. reappear, 5. retraced. 2. re/filled, 3. re/open, 4. re/placed, 5. re/traced. **P. 13.** Across—3. reopen, 5. replaced, 8. discontinue, 9. disagree, 10. disorder, Down—1. retraced, 2. reappear, 4. refilled, 6. dislike, 7. dishonest. **P. 14.** 1. unlucky, 2. unsafe, 3. unfinished, 4. untrue, 5. unhurt, 6. unafraid. **P. 15.** 1. impatient, 2. improper, 3. impure, 4. impossible, 5. impolite. **P. 16.** Across—2. untrue, 3. unfinished, 5. impolite, 6. impatient, 7. unlucky, 8. unsafe, Down—1. impure, 2. unafraid, 4. impossible, 6. improper, 7. unhurt. **P. 17.** dishonest—not truthful, reappear—come into sight again, unsafe—dangerous, impatient—restless, untrue—false, impure—not clean, retrace—go over lines on a paper again, disorder—mess, 1. dislikes, 2. refill, 3. unafraid, 4. impossible, 5. unhurt, 6. impolite, 7. replaced, disagree, 2. reopen, 3. dislike, 4. unlucky, 5. improper, 6. unafraid, 7. refill, 8. dishonest, 9. unhurt. **P. 18.** A—Builder, B—Painter, C—Trainer, D—Driver, E—Dancer. **P. 19.** 1. cheerful, 2. harmful, 3. careful, 4. wasteful, 5. colorful. 1. wonderful, 2. cheerful, 3. harmful, 4. careful, 5. wasteful. **P. 20.** Across—2. wonderful, 4. painter, 5. dancer, 7. colorful, 9. harmful, 11. cheerful, Down—1. trainer, 2. wasteful, 3. careful, 5. driver, 6. builder, 8. jeweler, 10. teacher. **P. 21.** 1. friendless, 2. careless, 3. helpless, 4. homeless, 5. nameless, 6. noiseless, 7. endless, 8. thoughtless, endless—without end, thoughtless—without thought, noiseless—without noise, careless—without care, friendless—without friends, helpless—without help, nameless—without a name, homeless—without a home. **P. 22.** 1. no lights, 2. quick happening, 3. order, 4. lack of strength, 5. good taste. 1. state of being slow, 2. state of being close, 3. state of being short, 4. state of being happy, 5. state of being ugly, 6. state of being lonely. **P. 23.** Across—2. friendless, 5. thoughtless, 9. careless, 10. noiseless, 11. nameless, 12. suddenness, Down—1. endless, 3. sweetness, 4. darkness, 6. homeless, 7. helpless, 8. weakness, 10. neatness. **P. 24.** 2. builder, 3. painter, 4. teacher, 5. trainer, 6. driver. 1. filled with wonder, 2 filled with cheer, 3. filled with harm, 4. filled with care, 5. filled with color. 1. homeless, 2. endless, 3. careless, 4. helpless, 5. friendless, 6. nameless, 2. slowness, 3. happiness, 4. neatness, 5. loneliness, 6. weakness, 7. sweetness, 8. closeness. **P. 25.** 1. things you can eat, 2. animals that eat only plants, 3. cake made from flour and spice. **P. 26.** 1. television or telly, 2. innings, 3. pitcher, 4. batter, 5. home plate. 6. home run, 7. fly ball. **P. 27.** 1. cirrus, 2. thunderhead, 3. cumulus, 4. thunderhead, 5. cirrus, 6. cumulus. A—5, 2, 3, 1, 4. B—2, 4, 5, 3, 1. **P. 28.** 1. b, 2. a, 3. a, 4. b, 5. a, 6. a. A special kind of machine. Doing a job without a person's help. **P. 29.** 1. land, 2. cook, 3. train, 4. spring, 5. land, 6. train, 7. cook, 8. spring. **P. 30.** 1. a place where students learn, 2. a large number of fish, 3. a flat dish for food, 4. the home base in baseball, 5. a large amount, 6. a piece of land, 7. something worn on the finger, 8. the sound of a bell, 9. the highest part, 10. a cover. A—4, 5, 2, 3, 1, B—5, 3, 1, 2, 4. **P. 31.** 2. hoe, 3. hive; 2, 4. hobby, 5. hockey, 6. hog; 2, 7. hive; 1. **P. 32.** school—a group of fish, spring—leap, land—soil, cook—bake, train—locomotive, spring—a time of year, land—set down an airplane, plate—flat dish, hive—a box for bees to live in, ring—sound of a bell. 1, 5, 4, 2, 3. Accept any reasonable responses. **P. 33.** 1. playground, 2. seesaw, 3. popcorn, 4. suitcase, 5. eyeglasses, 6. storyteller, 7. postcard, 8. scarecrow. 1. scarecrow, 2. eyeglasses, 3. playground, 4. storyteller, 5. seesaw, 6. popcorn, 7. postcard, 8. suitcase. **P. 34.** 2. raincoat, 3. tablecloth, 4. headache, 5. earring, 6. goldfish, 7. homework, 8. keyhole. Answers may vary. **P. 35.** Across—1. lifeboat, 4. rainbow, 6. goldenrod, 8. handbag, 9. firewood, 11. daylight, 13. daylight, 14. headlight. Down—2. iceberg, 3. playroom, 5. football, 7. outdoors, 10. railroad, 12. grapefruit. **P. 36.** seesaw, popcorn, scarecrow, suitcase, playground, goldfish, skyscraper, raincoat, tablecloth, eyeglasses, storyteller, postcard, headache, earring, keyhole, goldenrod, daylight, lifeboat, football. 1. headlight, 2. sailboat, 3. grapefruit, 4. playroom, 5. iceberg, 6. handbag, 7. firewood, 8. outdoors. **P. 37.** 1. thicket, 2. tune, 3. dashed, 4. foolish, 5. horrible, 6. creature. **P. 38.** 1. loping, 2. lair, 3. jungle, 4. peculiar, 5. huge, 6. leaped, 7. peril, 8. scurried. **P. 39.** 1. tossed, 2. confused, 3. valuable, 4. whispered, 5. damp. A—4, 5, 3, 2, 1, B—4, 2, 5, 1, 3. **P. 40.** 1. tune, dashed, 3. thicket, 4. horrible, 5. creature, 6. lair, 7. jungle, 8. leaped, 9. peril, 10. tossed, 11. valuable, 12. whispered, 13. damp. 1. foolish, 2. loping, 3. peculiar, 4. huge, 5. scurried, 6. confused. **P. 41.** 1. pane, 2. doe, 3. dough, 4. pain. 1. route, 2. pail, 3. pale, 4. root. **P. 42.** Across—2. beet, 5. allowed, 6. cent, 7. brake, Down—1. beat, 3. peace, 4. scent, 5. aloud, 7. break. Accept any reasonable responses. **p. 43.** 1. bow, 2. read, 3. dove, 4. dove, 5. read, 6. bow, 7. live, 8. live. **P. 44.** 1. doe, 2. dough, 3. pain, 4. pane, 5. beat, 6. beet, 7. aloud, 8. allowed, 9. piece, 10. peace, 11. scent, 12. cent, 13. brake, 14. break.